Getting To Know...

Nature's Children

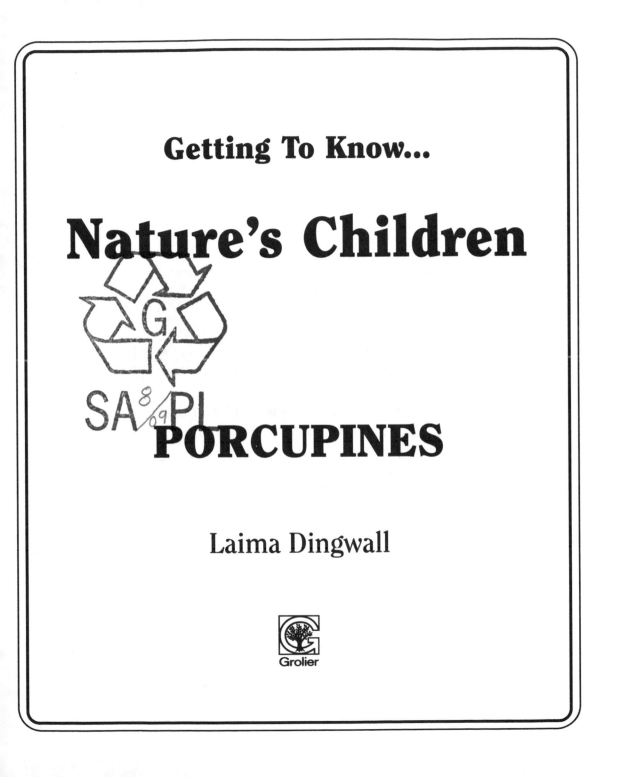

PORCUPINES

Laima Dingwall

Grolier

Facts in Brief

Classification of North American porcupines

    Class: *Mammalia* (mammals)

    Order: *Rodentia* (rodents)

    Family: *Erethizontidae* (tree-porcupine family)

    Genus: *Erethizon*

    Species: *Erethizon dorsatum* (Canada Porcupine)

            Erethizon epixanthum (Yellow-haired Porcupine)

World distribution. North American species exclusive to North America. Related species found in South America, Africa, Asia, India, and southern Europe.

Habitat. Pine and other forests; scrubland.

Distinctive physical characteristics. Ever-growing front teeth with orange-colored protective coating; body mostly covered with defensive quills underneath a layer of guard hairs.

Habits. Mostly solitary; active at night; when alarmed, bristles its quills and thrashes its tail so that quills fly out.

Diet. Twigs, branches, inner tree bark, and green vegetation—leaves, shrubs, flowers.

Edited by: Elizabeth Grace Zuraw
Design/Photo Editor: Nancy Norton
Photo Rights: Ivy Images

ISBN: 0-7172-8723-8

Have you ever wondered . . .

Try to imagine a walking pincushion. That's how the porcupine has been described. And no wonder! The porcupine has more than 30,000 sharp *quills,* needle-like spines that cover most of the top part of its body. Each one of the quills can be a painful weapon. But quills are only one chapter in a porcupine's life story.

Some campers know another chapter. They sometimes are awakened at night by the sound of loud gnawing. When they investigate, they discover that the culprit is none other than a porcupine, munching on a picnic table, a sign-post, or even a canoe paddle!

A walking pincushion that eats tables, sign-posts, and canoe paddles? As you'll discover, the porcupine is all of these things, but it's much more than that. It is also a shy, gentle, good-natured creature that just wants to be left alone.

The scientific name for the North American porcupine is Erethizon dorsatum. *That means "irritable back." An intruder that tangles with a porcupine often gets a quill attack that's more than just irritable!*

A Fast Learner

Tree-climbing is an important lesson for a baby porcupine to learn. In a tree, porcupines find safety, food, and a comfortable place to sleep.

To teach her baby how to climb, a mother porcupine climbs up a tree first. Then she chatters for her baby to join her. She keeps calling to encourage her little one as it slowly makes its way to the top.

A baby porcupine's first climb is usually its longest. That's because it might have to dig its claws into the tree several times before it gets a good grip. But with practice, the baby will soon be climbing up and down trees as easily as its mother.

In fact, a baby porcupine learns to climb trees within a week of its birth! Let's read on to find out more about this surprisingly agile animal.

The bottom of a porcupine's feet are covered with rough knobby skin that provides extra gripping power when the animal climbs trees.

This Porky is Not a Pig

Porcupines have sometimes been nicknamed "quill pig" or "porky." But the porcupine is not a pig. Perhaps it got its name because its nose is flat and snout-like, and it makes grunting sounds, like a pig.

Opposite page:
The name porcupine *comes from the Latin for "pig with thorns." But this animal's sharp quills and long claws make it anything but pig-like.*

The porcupine is a member of the rodent family. *Rodents* are animals with a certain kind of teeth that are especially good for gnawing. The porcupine's North American cousins include the mouse, rat, woodchuck, squirrel, gopher, and beaver.

Like all rodents, the porcupine has strong front teeth that never stop growing. But the porcupine doesn't have to worry about its teeth growing so long that it will trip over them! It keeps its teeth ground down by gnawing on tree bark.

North American porcupines have quilled cousins in Africa and Asia. But they are not related to two other quilled animals—the hedgehog and the spiny anteater.

A Fat Cat with Quills?

Next to the beaver, the porcupine is the largest rodent in North America. A full-grown male porcupine weighs 11-13 pounds (5-6 kilograms)—about the same as a big fat house cat. But some well-fed male porcupines weigh in at almost twice that weight. The average male porcupine measures about 3 feet (1 meter) from the tip of its nose to the end of its tail. The female is slightly smaller.

Where porcupines live in North America

Porcupine Country

Porcupines live in most parts of North America, except the southeastern United States and northern Alaska and the Yukon. Some porcupines live in dense forests, while others live in scrubland, often along rivers.

A porcupine is about the size of a house cat, but all those quills and fur make it look more roly-poly.

11

Tree Lover

Just think how handy it would be if your bed had a built-in kitchen cupboard. You would hardly have to disturb yourself at all when you wanted a snack—you'd just roll over and reach in. Well, porcupines can do just that! For them, a tree is both a resting place and a food supply.

Fortunately, the porcupine is well equipped for climbing trees. It digs its long curved claws into the bark, pushing with its rear paws and pulling itself up with its front paws. While climbing, it uses its broad sturdy tail as a prop. How? On the underside of its tail are stiff bristly hairs that dig into the tree's bark a bit like sandpaper.

Once it's up in the tree, the porcupine sits back and munches on tasty branches, bark, and leaves, or sprawls out and snoozes.

When a porcupine climbs down a tree, it uses its tail as a feeler to tell it when it has reached the ground.

On the Ground

When a porcupine wants to return to ground level, it shimmies down the tree tailfirst.

If you see a porcupine on the ground, you'll notice that it has short stubby legs. And it is slightly bow-legged and pigeon-toed. This gives the porcupine a clown-like, waddling walk or an awkward gallumping gallop if it's in a hurry.

However agile a porcupine may be in a tree, on the ground it moves with a slow and clumsy shuffle.

The Hairy Porcupine

A porcupine has three kinds of hair. In cold weather it grows an inner layer of thick underfur to keep in body heat. Much of this underfur falls out in late spring, when the weather warms up.

To keep out rain and snow, the porcupine's coat has *guard hairs,* long shiny coarse hairs that make up the outer layer of the coat. These guard hairs, brownish-black in color, not only keep the porcupine dry, they also make good *camouflage*—they blend in with the porcupine's surroundings so that enemies don't easily notice it.

But the porcupine is best known for its third kind of hair—its quills.

Even though its quills are excellent weapons, a porcupine prefers not to fight. If threatened, it would just as soon escape up a tree.

Hair That Hurts

You might find it a surprise to learn that a porcupine's quills are made of hardened hair. The point of each quill is covered with *barbs,* or tiny projections. These barbs lie flat against the quill when it is going into an intruder's flesh. But when the quill is being pulled out, the barbs open up a bit like an umbrella, and hook into the flesh. Ouch! Removing a quill can be very painful and difficult.

Every part of the porcupine's body is covered with these yellowish-white, barbed quills, except for areas on its face, belly, and the underside of its tail. Some quills can be as much as 4 or 5 inches (10 or 13 centimeters) long; others are the length of small pins.

A porcupine's hollow, tubed-shaped, and needle-sharp quills—shown here close-up—make good weapons.

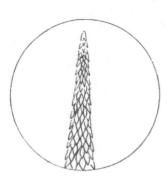

Closed barbs

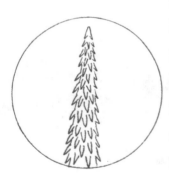

Open barbs

Stay Away—Or Else!

Most of the time you probably won't even notice a porcupine's quills. That's because they are usually covered by guard hairs as they lie flat against the porcupine's body. But once the porcupine is threatened or annoyed, muscles under its skin pull the quills so that they stand up. Then the porcupine is armed to defend itself.

Because most of the porcupine's quills are on its back and tail, it turns its back on enemies to protect itself. Then it stiffens its legs, arches its back, and lowers its head to the ground to defend its unprotected face and belly. As a last-minute warning it may chatter its teeth and hiss or even stomp its feet. Any animal that is foolhardy enough to ignore this "Stay Away" message is in for a nasty surprise.

When a porcupine loses a quill, a new one grows in to take its place. It takes between two and eight months for a new quill to grow in.

20

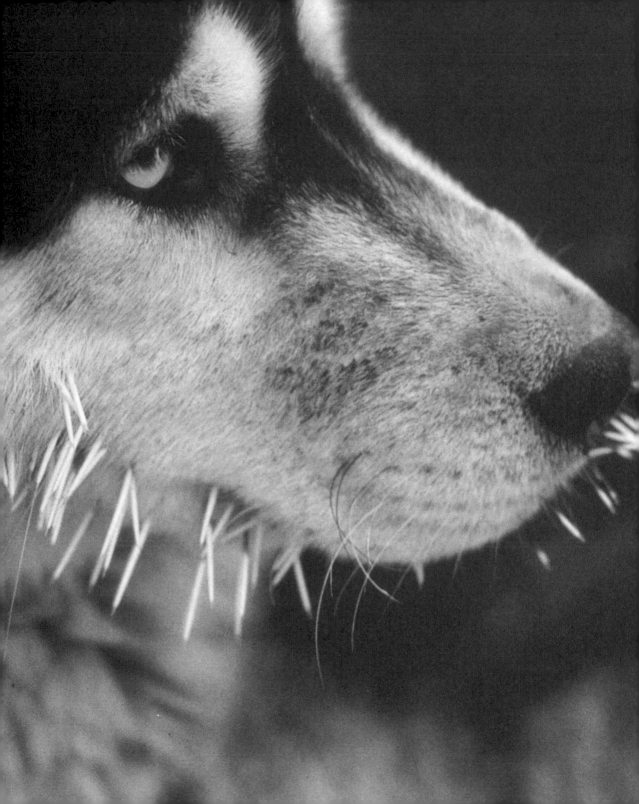

Ouch!

Some people think that a porcupine aims
and shoots its quills at enemies, but that's not
true. The quills are loosely attached to the
porcupine's skin, especially on the tail. When
the porcupine turns its back toward an enemy
and thrashes its tail back and forth to defend
itself, some of the quills fly out.

Most of these quills land on the ground and
do no harm. But if an enemy puts its nose or
mouth too close to a porcupine, it is almost
sure to leave with a faceful of quills. That's
not only painful; it can be dangerous. An
animal with quills in its mouth may not be
able to eat, and can starve to death.

With this coatful of painful weapons, it's
not surprising that the porcupine has few
enemies. But some animals, such as
wolverines, bobcats, and fishers, manage to
dodge the porcupine's quill-covered tail and
back, and flip the porcupine upside down.
That leaves the porcupine's quill-less
stomach unprotected.

A Porcupine Feast

What does a porcupine eat? Almost anything that grows! A typical porcupine menu might include leaves, flowers, and shrubs. In the summer, a porcupine will even wade belly-deep into a pond to feast on pond lilies and other water plants. If it's really hungry, it may paddle right across a pond in search of a tasty treat. Porcupines are good swimmers. Their hollow quills make a kind of natural life jacket.

But by far the porcupine's favorite foods are twigs and the inner bark of trees. North American porcupines prefer cone-bearing trees such as pines and firs. Unlike a beaver, which cuts down whole trees to get at the bark, a porcupine climbs a tree and chews on the branches. Sometimes, if a porcupine takes too big a bite, a branch will break off and fall to the ground. These "porcupine leftovers" help feed deer and rabbits in winter when other food is scarce. Porcupines eat so much bark during their lifetime that they themselves smell a bit like old wood or sawdust!

Opposite page:
A porcupine's favorite food is tree bark, but twigs and tender green plants make a fine snack, too.

Chompers To Gnaw With

If you had to bite chunks of bark off trees for your dinner, you'd need extra-strong teeth like the porcupine's. Luckily for the porcupine, its front bark-biting teeth never stop growing. Although they do get worn down from all that gnawing, more tooth grows in.

The porcupine's teeth are also very sharp. The outer part of the teeth has a tough orange-colored protective covering. As the porcupine bites off pieces of bark, the backs of the teeth wear down faster than the fronts. This helps to sharpen the tips of the teeth.

The porcupine has 16 other large flat teeth in its mouth for chewing and grinding its food.

Sturdy gnawing teeth make easy work for this porcupine when it peels the bark from an evergreen tree.

Strange Taste

Imagine how surprised some campers must be when they wake to find a porcupine munching on a pair of smelly sneakers. Eating stinky old shoes might sound pretty disgusting to you, but a porcupine finds them a delicious snack! That's because porcupines love anything that has been touched by perspiring human hands—or feet. When the perspiration dries, a trace of salt is left behind. Salt is a special treat to a porcupine.

Besides chomping on old running shoes, salt-loving porcupines have been known to eat canoe paddles, handles of tools, plywood signs, lawn furniture, and even the steering wheel of a car!

This porcupine is munching on the bark of a tree, but an even tastier treat would be a pair of old shoes.

Night Wanderers

The porcupine is a *nocturnal* animal, it is active mainly at night. That's when the porcupine wakes up and starts exploring. It waddles alone through the dark, looking for food. It may find a lush meadow where it can munch on flowers and leaves to its heart's and stomach's content, or it may spot a tasty-looking tree to gnaw. If a porcupine finds a good feeding spot it will go back night after night, following the same path it used the night before.

A favorite item in a porcupine's diet is bark. Porcupines prefer the bark of evergreen trees.

Daytime Sleepers

The porcupine snoozes for most of the day, usually up in a tree. If you look very carefully next time you take a walk in the woods, you just might see a sleeping porcupine stretched out on a branch with its legs dangling down.

But sleeping porcupines are usually difficult to spot. The porcupine's long guard hairs make it look like a clump of leaves or a bird's nest. Don't be tempted to climb up and take a closer look, though. If the porcupine is disturbed, it may back down the tree and thrash a tail full of quills against you.

You might not consider a treetop a good place for a snooze, but a porcupine considers it ideal.

A Nearsighted Sniffer

If you were nose to nose with a porcupine, you would see two dark little eyes staring back at you. And the porcupine is *nearsighted*—it could see you very well at that close range, but if you moved back several steps it might have trouble getting you into focus. However, thanks to its sensitive nose, the porcupine would still know you were there.

The porcupine relies on its keen sense of smell to help it find food. Since it searches for food at night when its eyesight is of little use, having a sharp nose makes a lot of sense. To put its super sniffer to best use, it walks with its nose to the ground or sits back on its haunches with its nose turned up to smell the air for food. When the porcupine finds something to eat, it usually gives the snack one last sniff before popping the food into its mouth.

Like a cat, a porcupine has whiskers growing out from the sides of its snout and cheeks. And much like a cat's whiskers, the porcupine's whiskers are sensitive feelers.

Love Songs and Dances

Opposite page:
Porcupines prefer living alone. A male and female porcupine spend only about a week together during mating season. Then each goes its own way.

Porcupines like to live by themselves. If two porcupines meet, they usually ignore each another. The only time porcupines are seen together is in the fall, during *mating season,* the time when animals *mate,* or come together to produce young. Then the usually shy male porcupine sets out to attract a female.

If two males cross each other's path during mating season, they may stand up on their hind legs and have a pretend fight. But after a few minutes, they lose interest in the fight and go off on their own to find mates.

To attract a mate, the male wanders through the forest singing a loud love song made up of hums, whines, grunts, and chatterings. The female, who finds these songs hard to resist, usually joins in with her own whines and coos to make a porcupine duet. The porcupine pair then dances together. They stand up on their hind legs and walk toward one another, whining and humming as they go. After sniffing each other, they put their paws on each other's shoulders and rub noses.

Wintertime Porcupines

Porcupines that live in cold climates do not *hibernate,* or go into a kind of heavy sleep in the winter. They are active all winter long. They rarely have to worry about where their next meal is coming from because food is as close as the nearest tree.

If the weather turns bitterly cold, a porcupine might curl up in a *den,* an animal home, abandoned by another animal. It might even bed down in a corner of an empty barn or rock cave.

Most of the winter the porcupine just tries to ignore the cold. It climbs up a tree where it is out of the snow and has its food supply right under its nose. Porcupines often spend weeks, even months, up the same tree, and even through severe cold.

Porcupines don't hibernate, so they can be active all winter long. A porcupine sometimes digs tunnels in the snow to get around.

Presenting the Baby Porcupine

When spring comes, it's time for a mother porcupine to find a sheltered spot in some shrubs, a hollow log, or a rock den to use as a nursery. A female has one baby porcupine, called a *cub,* in spring or early summer.

A newborn porcupine weighs about 1 pound (half a kilogram) and measures about 12 inches (31 centimeters) from its nose to its tail. Its eyes are open at birth, and it has eight teeth, including tiny front gnawing teeth. Half an hour after it's born, a baby porcupine can walk on its own.

The cub is born with a thick coat of soft black hair about as long as your pinky finger. Even its quills are soft, but in just a few hours they harden into small versions of its mother's quills.

Porcupine babies are well-developed at birth. In fact, a newborn porcupine is larger than a newly born black bear, even though the adult bear is many times larger than the adult porcupine.

Porcupine Lessons

The female porcupine raises her baby alone. When it is only a couple of days old, she begins to teach it how to climb up and down trees and to find food and shelter.

When it is not practicing tree climbing or food finding, the little porcupine snoozes under logs or among brush or low shrubs. Unlike its mother, who stays up her tree until dark, the young porcupine may wander around on the ground during the day, usually because it is hungry.

Even though a baby porcupine drinks its mother's milk until it is about six or seven weeks old, it starts to munch tender blades of grass, tree seedlings, herbs, and shrubs as early as two weeks after birth.

A little nudge from its mother helps a baby porcupine learn to climb a tree.

Playful Porcupines

If two little porcupines meet, they sometimes play-fight and chase one another in fun. This play-fighting helps the cubs learn how to defend themselves.

Baby porcupines, like most young animals, seem to love play—even if they're all alone. They have been seen walking stiff-legged and spinning around quickly in a circle like prickly tops.

Born in the spring or early summer, porcupine cubs learn survival techniques quickly, and reach complete maturity by fall of the year.

On Its Own

Mother and baby porcupine stay together for only about two months. They aren't seen together often, but they are always within calling distance of one another. The mother keeps track of her baby by chattering and making other noises. She "talks" to her baby when it is time to leave its daytime sleeping spot or when she wants it to climb a tree.

By fall the young porcupine is ready to go off on its own. If it has learned its porcupine survival lessons well, it will live to be about nine years old.

Other animals will keep a safe distance and other porcupines will leave it alone, but the young porcupine will not be lonely. It will take long snoozes during the daytime and explore for food at night, quite content to be on its own.

Words To Know

Barbs   Projections at the end of a porcupine quill that help it lodge in an intruder's flesh.

Camouflage   Coloring and markings on an animal that blend in with its surroundings.

Cub   Name of the young of various animals, including the porcupine.

Den   Animal home.

Guard hairs   Long coarse hairs that make up the outer layer of a porcupine's coat.

Hibernate   To fall into a kind of heavy sleep during the winter. When animals hibernate, their breathing and heart rates slow, and their body temperature goes down.

Mate   To come together to produce young.

Mating season   The time when animals mate.

Nearsighted   To be able to see things clearly only at close range.

Nocturnal   Active mostly at night.

Quills   Needle-like spines that cover most of the top part of a porcupine's body.

Rodent   An animal with certain kind of tccth that are especially good for gnawing.

Index

PHOTO CREDITS
Cover: Bill Ivy. **Interiors:** Bill Ivy, 4, 9, 28, 31. /*Valan Photos:* Joseph R. Pearce, 7; Stephen J. Krasemann, 16, 39; Michel Bourque, 19; Dennis W. Schmidt, 37. /*Ivy Images:* Lynn & Donna Rogers, 10, 25, 35, 42. /Barry Ranford, 13. /Tom W. Parkin, 15. /Leonard Lee Rue III, 21. /*Visuals Unlimited:* D. Cavagnaro, 22. /Thomas Kitchin, 27, 44. /Duane Sept, 33. /Vince Claerhout, 40.

Getting To Know...

Nature's Children

MALLARD DUCKS

Bill Ivy

Grolier

Facts in Brief

Classification of the Mallard Duck

    Class: *Aves* (birds)

    Order: *Anseriformes* (duck-shaped waterfowl)

    Family: *Antidae* (surface duck family)

    Genus: *Anas*

    Species: *Anas platyrhynchos*

World distribution. Widely distributed throughout North America, Europe, and Asia; in winter is found as far south as North Africa, India, and Southern Mexico.

Habitat. Shallow lakes, rivers, marshes; preferred seasonal habitat of prairie or woodland ponds and sloughs.

Distinctive physical characteristics. Male has a glossy greenish blue head and neck with white neck band; female is tawny brown.

Habits. Migration in small groups; preens to maintain waterproof feathers.

Diet. Water plants, grasses, seeds, frogs, insects.

Edited by: Elizabeth Grace Zuraw
Design/Photo Editor: Nancy Norton
Photo Rights: Ivy Images

ISBN: 0-7172-8724-6

Have you ever wondered . . .

Did you ever have a toy duck that you took into the bath with you? If you did, you've had a lot of company. And it's no wonder someone thought of ducks as bath toys. Ducks spend more time in the water than anywhere else.

At first sight, how a duck swims is a bit of a mystery. It bobs on the water like a cork and glides from place to place without seeming to move any part of its body. But if you could stick your head underwater and watch a duck swim past, you would soon solve the swimming duck mystery. Under the water's surface, the duck's huge yellow webbed feet paddle powerfully, moving the duck forward in a smooth glide.

There are more than a hundred different kinds of ducks in the world. One of the most beautiful and widespread of them is the Mallard. Let's unravel some other duck mysteries by finding out more about the Mallard.

Mallards are the most common wild ducks. Like all ducks, they spend most of their time in the water.

Meet a Mallard Duckling

A mother Mallard sits on her nest, warming her eggs for about four weeks. Then suddenly one day she hears a sound. It's a tiny "peep peep" coming from one of the eggs. The mother duck's long wait is over—her eggs are about to *hatch,* break open so that the babies inside can emerge.

After a few minutes a small hole appears in the noisy egg…then a crack. Finally the shell splits in two and a brown and yellow duckling steps out, its feathers sticking up in wet spikes. Weak from the effort of breaking out of the shell, it sits quite still and looks around bewildered. What will life be like for this baby Mallard when it grows up?

A Mallard's eggs are dull yellow or greenish.

Male and Female

You certainly don't have to be an experienced bird-watcher to tell a male Mallard from a female. They look very different.

Few birds are as beautiful as the male Mallard, or *drake*. He has a handsome glossy green head, a bright yellow bill, a narrow white collar, and a purplish-chestnut breast. As a finishing touch, two tail feathers curl up and rest on top of his sleek black and white tail. The drake is slightly larger than the female. He may measure up to 27 inches (70 centimeters) in length and weigh as much as 3 pounds (1.3 kilograms).

In contrast to the drake, the female Mallard has a rather dull feathered costume. She is a mottled brown and white with an orange and brown bill. The male Mallard is brightly colored to attract a mate. The female is dull colored so that she doesn't attract attention when she is looking after her eggs.

Like other ducks, Mallards pick a new mate each year.

Telltale Talk

Before you even see the *plumage,* or feather covering, of a Mallard pair, you can tell a male and female apart. How? They have different voices. The female has a loud "quack quack" call, and she's more talkative than the male. When the male "talks," he has a faint, high-pitched quack.

Handsome, swift, and colorful are just a few ways to describe the Mallard drake.

Waterproof and Warm

Imagine swimming all day without getting cold or wet. Ducks can do that. They have two layers of feathers to keep them warm and dry. Next to their bodies is a layer of light fluffy feathers called *down*. This traps warm air close to the duck's skin. Smooth outer feathers act like a shield and keep out cold air and water.

To make its outer feathers extra waterproof, a duck uses its broad beak to coat them with oil from a gland at the base of its tail. A *gland* is a part of an animal's body that makes and gives out a substance. This waterproofing must be done several times a day. Without this protective film of oil, the inner layer of down would become waterlogged and the duck could drown.

Both male and female Mallards have a streak of iridescent blue on their wings.

"Like Water Off a Duck's Back"

You can see for yourself how the Mallard's waterproofing works. Find a feather and gently apply a thin coat of vegetable oil to both sides of it with your fingers. Now sprinkle the feather with water. The water beads up on the surface and rolls off very easily. Under the layer of oil the feather stays dry because water and oil don't mix.

Now you know why people use the expression "like water off a duck's back" when they mean that something happens easily and naturally.

At one time, the name Mallard referred only to the colorful male. Now the name is used for both the male and the female.

Duck Territory

The Mallard is the world's most common wild duck. You can travel through North America, Europe, Asia, and even parts of Africa, and you're sure to find these beautiful birds.

You'll usually spot Mallards near fresh water. They will happily settle next to a lake, river, marsh, or pond. Mallards are especially fond of tiny seasonal ponds, marshes, and swampy inlets.

In the wild, Mallards are extremely cautious, and it's very difficult to get near them. But some Mallards live in city parks and often become quite tame and lazy. They're used to having people around them, and they take handouts from park visitors. If you have never seen a Mallard before, a park with a pond or stream in your town or city might be a good place to look.

Mallards prefer to make their home in the fresh waters of ponds, lakes, and marshes, rather than the salty water of oceans.

Choosing a Mate

Early spring is the season when Mallards *mate,* or come together to produce young. Mallards choose a new mate every year. To attract and impress females, the drakes show off their beautiful colors. Often they put on a water ballet. A drake will bow to a female Mallard and dip his bill in the water. There is much nodding, splashing, and spraying. He might even rear up and spread his wings, as if to say, "Look how handsome I am."

Sometimes two or more males fight over a female. Usually no one is seriously hurt. The winner and his mate become an inseparable pair. They feed, swim, and play together.

If this female Mallard finds this drake irresistible, she might choose him as a mate by touching him with her bill.

Nesting Time

Opposite page:
Usually built in a secluded spot and always lined with fluffy down feathers, a Mallard nest holds eight to twelve eggs.

After a Mallard has chosen a mate, the pair looks for a good place to build a nest. Most often Mallards choose a secluded spot on the ground, not too far from water. If good nesting sites are hard to find, they will make do with whatever they can find. Mallards have been known to nest in such unexpected places as an abandoned crow's nest high in a tree, on top of a haystack, and even on a roof.

The nest, built by the female only, is made of twigs, reeds, and dry grass. For added warmth, she plucks some down feathers from her breast and uses them to line her nest. In this cozy cushion she lays eight to twelve pale yellow or greenish-gray eggs. When the last egg has been laid, the mother duck nestles over them to keep them warm and safe. This is called *brooding*. The father duck protects the nest against enemies for about a week. Then he leaves to spend the summer with the other drakes.

The Long Wait

For 28 days the mother duck patiently sits on the eggs. By keeping them warm, the ducklings inside will grow. From time to time she rolls the eggs over with her bill so that every part of each egg is warmed. While she is brooding, the mother Mallard's colors blend perfectly with her surroundings. This *camouflage,* or blending in with surroundings, helps hide the Mallard mother from enemies and keeps the nest safe.

Each time the mother duck leaves the nest to feed and *groom,* or clean herself, she covers her eggs with feathers, grass, and twigs. This keeps the eggs warm and hidden from hungry animals such as crows, skunks, raccoons, and weasels. These *predators,* animals that hunt other animals for food, might try to rob the nest while the mother is gone.

If a mother Mallard is disturbed or frightened off the nest, she may desert her eggs. This is one reason that you should never disturb a bird while it is nesting.

Opposite page: *A nest of eggs or the new hatchlings are called a* clutch.

Hatch Day

It's not easy for the ducklings to break out of their eggs, but they are persistent. To help them, each duckling has an *egg tooth,* a hard sharp growth at the end of its bill. Using this egg tooth like a miniature hammer, the first baby begins to break out of its shell. Before long there is a nestful of surprised looking brown and yellow ducklings.

Egg tooth on duckling's bill

The ducklings huddle together in the nest seeking warmth. The mother Mallard nuzzles her babies and covers them with her wings. She does this to protect them and keep them warm. But as she nestles over them, some of the oil from her wings brushes off onto their down and helps to waterproof them until their own oil glands begin to work. Within an hour of birth, the hatchlings are fluffy and dry and fully rested.

Ducklings huddle together to keep warm. When the mother Mallard returns to the nest, she'll cover her babies with her wings.

To the Water

Have you ever heard the expression, "like a duck takes to water"? People say this about someone who shows a natural ability for something. And if you were to watch a duckling take its first swim, you'd see exactly why this saying came about. Ducklings don't need any swimming lessons. They're naturally at home in the water.

As soon as the ducklings' down feathers have dried, their mother leads them to the water's edge.

Ducklings follow their mother to the water when they're only a day or two old.

The First Swim

Slowly the mother Mallard wades out into the water and her little family follows. Even though the water is cold and unfamiliar to the baby ducks, they just start paddling. Immediately they discover that their brown and orange webbed feet are perfectly designed for swimming.

A duck's webbed foot

Ducks are not fast swimmers. The mother likes to cruise along at a leisurely pace, but even so, the ducklings often have to paddle with all their might to keep up. The mother duck stops now and then to check for stragglers among her family.

Even when they're just a few days old, baby Mallards swim confidently. Baby ducks don't need lessons. Swimming comes to them naturally.

Big Eaters

The Mallard family stays among the reeds along the shore. These provide some cover from hungry predators such as hawks and big fish. And there's plenty of food in these shallow waters, making them a mighty fine smorgasbord for ducks.

Opposite page:
Ducklings spend their first three months with their mother, feeding, bathing, preening, or smoothing their feathers—or just plain loafing.

Have you ever been to a smorgasbord? If you have, you know that it offers such a huge variety of foods that you hardly know where to begin. You usually end up sampling a little of everything. This is exactly what a Mallard duckling does.

Ducklings are born with huge appetites and are eager to try all the new foods around them. Seeds, leaves, and stems of pond weeds are among their favorite foods. Insects, worms, and tadpoles make tasty side dishes. And for dessert, maybe some snails or fish eggs will nicely top off a meal. This menu may not sound very appetizing to you, but it's a feast to a duckling.

Dabbling Ducks

Finding food is hard work for ducklings. They have to learn to "dabble" for their food the way grown-up ducks do. Dabbling ducks tip their tails straight up and stretch their necks under the water. In this way they can reach food just below the water's surface. Dabbling ducks find most of their food in shallow water.

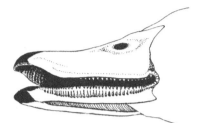

Close-up of Mallard bill

A Mallard's bill is a perfect tool for uprooting and eating underwater plants. It's a bit like a sieve—it traps food and lets the water drain out. As they grow older, the young ducklings learn to swallow gravel, sand, and shells. This grit may make up as much as half of a duck's stomach contents. Why do ducks eat such odd things? There's a practical answer. Ducks don't have teeth like yours. The rough material they eat helps to grind up their food.

It's easy to spot a dabbling duck: Its head goes underwater and its tail goes straight up.

Danger!

The lakes and ponds where the young ducks grow up are home to many duckling enemies. Perhaps the most fearsome are the Snapping Turtles that sometimes lie in wait in shallow water, partially buried in the mud. Lurking in deeper waters are large, hungry fish such as Pike and Muskies. They also like a tasty meal of duckling.

There are predators waiting on land, too, and even in the air. Foxes, skunks, raccoons, hawks, and crows are quick to pounce on the fuzzy ducklings if they get a chance.

The mother Mallard does her best to keep her ducklings safe. If an enemy approaches, she may try to lure it away from her young. To do this, she may pretend she has broken a wing. Quacking loudly and dragging her "broken" wing, she leads the enemy away. When it's safe, she's quick to hurry back to her little family.

Quacking loudly, flapping her wings, and stretching out her neck in a threatening jab—these are some of a mother Mallard's ways of saying "Stay away!"

New Clothes

By the time they are about a month old, the ducklings have *molted,* they have lost their baby down, and have grown soft brown and gray feathers. At the end of the summer the ducklings molt again. What a mess this makes! Clouds of feathers fly in every direction when the young ducks groom or shake themselves.

When the change is complete, the young females look just like their mother. The young males look more like their father, but they won't grow their full colorful adult male feathers until their second year.

The mother Mallard raises her family by herself. The father leaves shortly after the eggs are laid, and gathers with other drakes. The males lose their colorful feathers at that time—so fast, in fact, that they can't fly for two or three weeks. The drakes don't grow their dazzling colored plumage again until the next mating season.

Earning Their Wings

When the ducklings are one to two months old, they begin to learn how to fly. Their new wing feathers make their wings seem large compared to the rest of their bodies. Most waterfowl must take a running start before they are airborne, but not Mallards. Their powerful wings allow them to spring straight up into the air in an explosive vertical take-off.

It takes some practice, but eventually the young ducks master the art of taking off, flying, and landing. Soon they'll be able to fly at speeds of nearly 60 miles (100 kilometers) an hour for short bursts. This is as fast as many cars travel on highways.

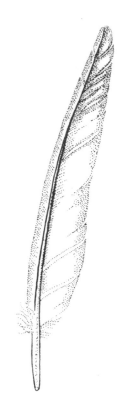

Mallard feather

Like all Mallards, these spring straight up into the air from a sitting position. Other kinds of ducks have to patter along the water's surface before becoming airborne.

Two Homes

Mallard ducks that nest on northern lakes must fly south to warmer winter homes when the weather turns cold in the fall. If they stayed in the North, they would starve because the ice that forms on lakes and ponds would cut them off from their food supply. This seasonal move from one place to another is called *migration*.

Not all ducks migrate. If the weather is not too cold, or if they can find enough food and open water, some ducks stay where they are for the winter.

Ducks don't mind the cold. They can live in snowy places just so long as the ponds and marshes don't freeze over, cutting off their supply of food.

The Long Journey South

When autumn comes in the North, the days become cool and the nights are chilled by cold frosts. As soon as ice begins to form on ponds and rivers, the Mallards can delay no longer. It's time to migrate to the warm wetlands of the South. Some Mallards fly almost 3,000 miles (5,000 kilometers) on this incredible journey to friendlier climates.

Ducks have none of the travel aids that people take for granted. They have no maps, compasses, or weather forecasters to direct and help them. Yet somehow they know the exact paths they must take. Year after year ducks use the same routes, called *flyways,* between their northern nesting grounds and their southern winter homes. The ducks fly together in groups high in the sky. Often they form a long V behind the leader.

Ducks are excellent flying birds. Mallards can move at speeds of 60 miles per hour over a short distance.

A Dangerous Time

Ducks face many dangers during the long trip south. They often have to travel through rain, wind, and storms. Predators, droughts, and hunters claim many lives. Fortunately, some safe places, called *sanctuaries,* have been set aside for the ducks. Here, hundreds of ducks can safely rest and feed. If there is no sanctuary around, a flock of Mallards may stop in a farmer's field and feed on grain and corn left over from the harvest.

By the time their migration is over, some of the Mallards will have traveled as far south as Mexico, Central America, or the West Indies. Once at their destinations, they spend the winter in these warm places.

A ground cover of snow makes food searches more difficult, but ducks can stay in cold climates if they can find enough food.

Summer Homes

In early spring, the Mallards begin the long flight north to their summer homes. They usually arrive at their nesting grounds in late March or early April. Soon after they return, they start to look for nesting sites. It won't be long before the "peep peep" of little ducklings is heard again.

Fine Feathered Friends

The Mallard has adapted itself to human ways better than any other duck. Mallards have even learned to like the same foods that people do and to help themselves to the apples, potatoes, peas, and corn growing in farmers' fields. But ducks also help people by eating huge numbers of mosquito larvae every year. That means fewer pesky mosquito bites for us.

What a fascinating bird the Mallard is! And how fortunate we are that they are so plentiful in both the country and city. Perhaps the next time you see a Mallard, you'll stop to think of what an adventurous life it leads.

Words To Know

Brooding   A mother Mallard's way of keeping her eggs safe and warm by sitting on her nest.

Camouflage   Coloring and markings on a bird or animal that blend in with its surroundings.

Clutch   The eggs laid by a mother Mallard and the ducklings that hatch from the eggs.

Dabbling   A Mallard's method of tipping its tail straight up and stretching its neck under the water to get food below the water's surface.

Down   Very soft, fluffy feathers.

Drake   A male duck.

Egg tooth   A tooth-like point on a duckling's bill used to help it crack out of its shell.

Flyway   A migration route used by birds.

Gland   A part of the body that makes and gives out a substance.

Grooming   The activity of an animal in cleaning and caring for itself.

Hatch   To emerge from an egg.

Mate   To come together to produce young.

Migration   A seasonal move from one place to another.

Molt   To shed one set of feathers and grow another.

Plumage   The entire covering of feathers on a bird.

Predator   An animal that hunts other animals for food.

Preening   The activity of Mallards and other birds that includes smoothing and caring for their feathers.

Sanctuaries   Special safe fields and ponds where ducks and other birds cannot be hunted.

Index

PHOTO CREDITS
Cover: Bill Ivy. **Interiors:** *Tom Stack & Associates:* Thomas Kitchin, 4. /James Richards, 7, 22.
/*Ivy Images:* Lynn & Donna Rogers, 8, 16, 39; Robert McCaw, 32. /*Valan Photos:* M. J.
Johnson, 11. /*Visuals Unlimited:* W. Ormerod, 12; Dick Thomas, 44. /Bill Ivy, 15, 21, 26-27, 35,
36. /Wayne Lankinen, 19. /George E. Peck, 24, 40. /V. Claerhout, 28. /*Lowry Photography*, 31.
/*Canada In Stock / Ivy Images:* Gary Crandall, 43.